Poems and Short Stories

For
Black
Pearls

Dedicated to my parents,

Demaris Carter
James Carter

And in remembrance of my
grandfather,

Samuel W. Robinson

This is for all of the
beautiful black pearls.

CONTENTS

CONTENTS

Smoking Mirrors

Smoking Mirrors

Like darkness hiding from light...
fear, shivering, holding myself tightly...
See, it's just me.
It's always been me fighting this war.
My soul is a democracy
and I've been elected to battle my biggest enemy
my reflection, which I occasionally show little affection
like most young colored girls.

I smile in the looking glass
and then slash myself into a million pieces.
This is what they didn't teach us.
That one day we'd fall out of love with ourselves and would
have to start all over again, embracing our names, loving the skin we're in.
Beauty has no eyes. 24/7, 365 it's blind.
So, no, it can not see the tears we think we hide.
Such a faulty disguise. We bathe in our lies, drowning in our own dirty bath water of hurt.

Born into curses
whipped traditions
welts on our backs
WE ARE IN PAIN!!!
Driving ourselves insane because we can't understand
why no one loves us.

Too small
Too big
Too skinny
Too fat
Small lips
Big eyes
Irregular feet
Tiny thighs

We are perfection made from the saliva of God.
A spitting image.
Who are we to say we are ugly or unwanted?
Beauty has no eyes.
Yes, Beauty is blind, so even she can't see the tears that we think we hide.

Bitter Taste of Loneliness

It stalks her like a shadow,
haunting her consciousness and perverting her dreams,
clustering her mind and muffling
the deadly screams.

Abandoned like an aborted fetus (barely with all 10 toes),
misery impregnates her and, sadly, she's beginning to show.
Standing tall with her head limp,
an outcast afraid of the boisterous backlash.

It is loneliness, a fear of loneliness,
the aloneness of loneliness that
erases her memory of happiness... of truth.

Dared Not to Love

All I keep hearing is the
crying and weeping.
I keep feeling
hard kicks at the pit of my gut.

"Mommy, Mommy, save me."

I can't help you.
I'm not wise enough to teach you about life.
Not strong enough to pull you up by your bootstraps
or gentle enough to tuck you in at night.

I am not good enough to love you.
I am not good enough to hold you.

I want you to know your Daddy
and fall asleep to his lullabies.
I don't want to tell you he never wanted you
and have to wipe the tears from your eyes.
I can't bring myself to wear that disguise.

"Mommy, Mommy, save me."

I know you want to live, baby.
But so do I, yet I'm not bold enough to bring you into this world.

I'm too ashamed for us to see eye to eye.
My eyes too beaten, broken, buried
under pounds of lies, fear, selfishness and discontent.

This world wasn't made for you, so enjoy the darkness.
Sit at the foot of God and tell him to forgive me,
and to love you fiercely -unlike how I dared not to love you.

Black Pearls

She stands alone in the background,
dancing to the melody of an eerie self-written tune.
No one sees the way she sways,
nor do they smell the strong scent of her perfume.

Loosely around her neck
is a string of black pearls
that were once white when her mama gave them to her
as a little girl.

She's been east of south and north of west
and not once did she stop to rest.
A lone gypsy
traveling through time,
squeezing past her demons,
drowning in tequila,
sinking in sliced limes.

Poor thing.
No one told her life has no chaser.
No backspace, no white out,
no jumbo erasers.

She's been etched and sketched.
Her glass house, yep, that's been shattered by stones.
No belongings left, but her weak bones.

black girl, your black pearls are falling off the string.

Untitled

I planted you deep down in the soil.

I gave you light. Water. Love.
But you never grew.
They never do.

Perhaps my thumb isn't green enough?

Up and Go

You messed up when you turned on that TV.
Took a good look at that woman and realized she wasn't me.

It may have been love at first sight, when you saw her shimmering eyes,
long hair and slim thighs.

"Why have you been wasting your time with me?"

And right at that moment, you dropped all your things.
I nearly died when I saw you jump inside the TV screen.

You wandered, and I cried.
You searched, while I lied,
telling everyone you'd be back soon.

I spent nights howling at the moon
and deeply wishing on the brightest star
for your return.

But I didn't realize you would be back so soon.
Look at you. You look broken and used.
Pockets all empty, and your heart, well, that's bruised.

I guess she didn't make you feel so swell
like you thought she would.
Oh, she didn't make you laugh the way that I could?

I think your eyes were too big for your heart.
My heart's too big for your hurt.
So darling dear, I can't take you back
although it pains me so.
But that's how it works when you just
up and go.

Love Song

I get along without you very well

Skips over and over in my head like a scratched record.
The repetition of being alone
Mocks me
And I shutter,
Closing my eyes tightly
And grinding my teeth.

"Have you gotten along without me?"

The days just don't seem the same.
The sun and the moon resemble each other
More and more, and though I try to move along,
I keep hearing that
Same sad song.

No Use

What's the use of calling if
you can't hear me when I say, "I love you?"

There's no point in holding me tightly,
if you can't feel my warmth.

Why do you keep returning?

What do you want from me,
if all I can give you is love?

Haiku
(cross your legs)

lil' girl cross your legs
and ignore him when he begs
love lives in silence

How Long?

How long is forever?
Does it last as long as the sunset
or does it die with the moon?

Does it stay like true love
or fade like friendships do?

Forever doesn't seem to be a very long time; yet, whenever
I think of forever, I still dream of your eyes.

When He Touches Me

When he touches me,
my body shakes.
My heart cracks in pieces like
Caribbean earthquakes.

His hands slither around my neck
like a thousand garter snakes.
What's it going to take
for him to stop for a second,
take a glance down at his gold watch,
and realize how long he's been
gripping my wrists?

Nearly digging into my veins,
when he touches me,
I fall to my knees
and let him walk over me.
He pulls me by my reins.
His words whip and rip my back.

He touches me gently, and I melt like
candles left lit over night.

You break me and fix me
and break me again.

Haiku

he tries to heal me
however the pain still stays
keeping me from me

19

Stay

You could've at least brought flowers,
before you said goodbye.
I would've planted them in our garden and prayed that
they'd grow tall enough to reach you in the sky.

But you left, and I was too afraid to say goodbye.
Hoping that my hesitations would leave room for your
reservations, and maybe you'd decide to stay....
You left anyway.

You could've brought me flowers.
You know, just to soften the blow.
I would've left them in the darkest part of my soul
and in the silence, they'd glow.

Your love is like spring…

pouring rain and weathered tulips.

Pollinated.

It causes my eyes to itch, my nose to run, and for me
to let out a

biiiiiiiiiiiiiiig sneeze.

Valentine's Day

I've left a path of crumbs,
of which composed my heart,
in a trail behind me.
If anyone wants to find my love,
the quest should be quite easy.

Love
Supreme

You Are

You are a beautiful flower
You are a beautiful flower
You are a beautiful flower
Such a flower—the rarest thing I've ever seen.

I'd like to grow a whole patch of you,
so I can smell you as you sweetly bloom.
And If I could, I'd plant me too.
Under the dirt, I'd hold on to you.

Have Ya?

Have you ever truly heard God?
I believe I have.

I'm still listening.
All yours. All ears...

He told me to find my balance, because I'm so close
to slipping and falling into sinking sand.

Have you ever truly felt God's hands?
I believe I have.
And, gently,
He pushed me into

You.

Honey Sweet
Mahogany, Pt. II

Sunburned faces with lashes on their backs.
Pricked fingers from the fabric of the shirts they lacked.

Working to the rhythm of repeated hymns
and praying to have the strength by noon.

Enlightened, when the sun shined brown just for them.
Broken chains. Running against the wind.

Boomerang

& just like that you came back to me.
A feeling of magnetic energy.
So warm, you rested in my hands
and when I pressed you against blank pages,
you bled
truth
love
heartache
and, most of all, joy.

All In Love

I don't know what you see in me,
but I thank you for not being blind.
I, however, am having a hard time loving with open eyes.
But if I lend you my hand, promise to be my guide.

Help me forget about all of the whatnots and
should have beens.
Now I know what it all really means.
Love is kind and quiet and careful and so brutally honest.

Thank you for showing me what I'm missing.
And although I may not be ready, I'll one day soon fight the fear.
I'm a work in progress, but you seem not to care.

All in love is fair.

Brown Man

You are beautiful
and brilliantly designed,
from the bushiness of your eyebrows
to the strength of your thighs.

I love you, brown man.
I don't know how often you're being told
that you are an amazing treasure
beaming like gold.

Courageous like jungle cats;
I love to hear you roar.
My cup runneth over with love
and you keep pouring me more.

Black Brotha,
I adore
Your smile
Your laugh

And even your stubborn pride.

Your integrity
Your quietness
Your mystery

Your disguise.

Just A Thought

lying in a field of sunflowers,
the petals fall, like raindrops, upon my face.
brushing against my forehead and smooching my cheeks.

I want to grow as tall as the sunflowers and shine as
brightly as they do.
then, just maybe you'd notice my light, because everyday
I'd shine on you.

An Ordinary
Love Poem

It's getting late.
The clock pauses.
Endless time is moving.
Still,
I feel no motions of the seconds
minutes
hours
days
This is love, man.

A Love Supreme

Yah,
I'm thinking sweet Sunday afternoon.
Coltrane busting through...
Soft, furious, bouncing melodies leave me
Wanting that love...supreme.

for the forgotten
black souls

I have no magical dust up my sleeves,
so I cannot bring back Martin or Malcolm or Coretta or Rosa or
Dorothy or Abernathy or Garvey or Stokely or
Huey and the raging Panthers.
But I thank God for their existence and the souls they saved.

I won't pour out an ounce of liquor or create a makeshift vigil
because surely there's no time
and perhaps the idea would be in vain.
Although our black is still beautiful,
hidden beneath the dye lies pain.

So this is for the mahogany, sable voices that pierced our hearts in
rebuttal and resistance.
Soaring eagles, leading packs of doves
to a land that was promised.

This is for you, my brother
For you, my sister
For you, my mother
For you, my father
For you, my ancestors

For you, my child.

ta dum ta dum ta
ba bop ba bop sweee leee
my love for you is jazz.

Rummaging through the heaviness of your confession
burdens me to think and accept you, but
with aggression, I open my heart
And butterflies soared from the pits of my soul
And my eyes fogged with your essence
And my fingers shook and the hairs on my arms rose
And my lips trembled.

Ta dum ta dum ta
Ba bop ba bop sweee leee
my love for you is
Jazz.

Cat & Mouse

You're so stubborn,

        But

            I

Am persistent.

Who Will Cry?

And this is for the lost children
who never made it home.

Whose fathers
grip flashlights
in the middle of the night,
shouting their child's names over and over and over
only to hear his echo in return.

Who will cry for the lost children
who didn't live
to blow out seven birthday candles
better yet see a sweet sixteen?

Surely not the government
who let killers off free.

He didn't mean it,
let's blame it on insanity.

Will you cry for the child
whose lonely tooth lay beneath
his cold pillow?

Whose mother's head hangs low like weeping willows?

If not you and I, tell me, who will cry?

A Blues for You

In the far and dreary distance,
I hear your faint tune.
A melody so sweet, soft, subtle
like blues.

A blues calling for me, whispering and whimpering my name.
I follow your direction, as the bouncing notes keep me sane.
Tapping lightly across my heart like the drizzles that fall on my
window pane.

I'm searching for that blue blues.
I wanna scat to your riffs and snap to your snare,
kick my heels off and two step.

Run in the rain—drip
ping wet in your blues.

I want to go back to my roots.
I got too many cavities from the sugar coats of America.
Give me the
reds
yellows
blacks and greens.
Play the rhythm of the drum
that my ancestors once played.
I wanna go back to my rooooots!
Deep
O
W
N
where the seeds were planted and forgotten, and
where my people fell through the cracks of separation.
Take
us back black.
Take
me back black.

Natural Love

A joyful sound has awakened me.
A sound of pouring rain and buzzing bees.
The voice of the blowing breeze and of the falling leaves.
I hear my name.
Nature's calling me.

A peaceful invitation that I dare not decline.
The sun so bright, nearly blinding my eyes.
But it is so beautiful-the colors of the wind.
The purples, the yellows, the greens
all reflect the image of you,
and it seems that I can sit out here all day
to simply bask in your presence, in your strong spirit.
You are, naturally, a gift from God.

I'm not sure if you knew how much you meant to me
because, knowing me, I was too shy to really say.
And although you can't hear me now,
I'd like to tell you anyway...

You were like a rare flower
that only bloomed in the dawn.

God, I loved the mystery of you.

Each moment we shared
was like morning,
quiet and new.

I embraced your silence
and observed the wrinkling of your hands.
You were like time.

And quickly, like the seconds, you faded
and I watched your name disappear in the sands.

When I was a young girl,
you'd kiss me on my cheeks and pinch them really hard.

Sometimes I can still feel the sting.
And when I do, I close my eyes tightly,
imagining you here with me.

I'm so sorry, but

I was too afraid to see you dying
I was too afraid to face such a painful goodbye.
I wanted to remember you happy and healthy and

I wanted to remember you alive.

The
Phoenix

You know you?
I mean really know you.
Not just "my favorite color is blue" you.

You know the rhythm of your heart?
Do you hear it while you sleep?
How does it beat? In simple measures?
Or is it a complicated melody?

You know you?
I mean *really* know you.
Not just "my favorite color is blue" you.

Rebirth

Cleansed in rivers like Jordan.
She sings new harmonies with
the birds.

Dripping milk and honey from her lips,
she spins in circles, letting
warm wind brush against her skin like
sheets of silk.

Homage to My Legs
(inspired by Lucille Clifton)

Thick branches of foundation
keep me balanced when this world gets shaky.
Milk chocolate smooth legs
of a Swahili queen,
singing sweet tribal sounds,
as each foot hits the ground.

Sweet like cinnamon sticks and
patient like the art of ballet
moving along to the rhythm of my hips,
each second they sway.

Tantalizing legs that have walked through
sunshine and rain.
Legs that have hit the ground in misery and
kneeled in pain.

These legs have stood tall,
Walking past bowed heads and wet lips.
Sprinkling spring dew, gracefully with each stride.

Moving slowly like the river (my soul is deep like the river),
I find my mind in perfect peace, wrapped in the breath of
God.
HE has delivered me.
Hurt falls from my body like small pebbles of sand.
My heart beats faster at the feeling of his hand.
Forgiveness, redemption, freedom.
The holiness of Jesus—his voice soft as a lullaby—rocks me
like a newborn in the still of the night.
I've found God
And he feels
gooooooooooooooooood.

Daddy Made Me
(secrets of broken-hearted girls)

Tammy

Is it really my fault that I can't live
without validation from a man?

I've never been held softly by strong hands.
Never knew daddy. He had other plans.

I wanna find that big bubbling love that will fill the void.
A love so loud, it'll drown out the noise.

Liz

They tell me I'm beautiful, but I don't believe them.
No girl will ever be beautiful for tossing and turning with different men.
My heart aches and clatters like tin.

Make me feel beautiful like I'm your baby girl.
Make me believe you brought me into this world.

Kenya

Love me and need me more than he ever did.
He just wanted loose women to follow home to their beds.
And I thought, well, maybe if I was like them then Daddy would find his way back
to me and he'd see the type of woman he made me be.

Alicia

Each night my tears would fall slowly like
melting wax.
Can't you see that I just want to be wanted, loved, and to be needed?

And even if I'm mistreated,
it still feels like I have a purpose,
but I'm tired of being seen as worthless.

And so it *is* my fault

that I let men use me
rip my heart out my chest and
verbally abuse me.

Tammy

I never let the pain go.
I just hid it real good underneath the cushion of
my shoes.

Liz

Standing on a crumbling foundation,
bringing me to my knees,
begging for salvation-

Kenya

it is me to blame for feeling sorry for myself,
for not finding the back door out of hell.

Alicia

Get this mask off my face.
It's so tight. I. can't. breathe!

Liz

I want to feel free
rolling wildly in sharp blades of grass,
cutting me deeply to my core.

Kenya

Let the pain trickle and seep into the soil.

Alicia

And let it dry like that festered raisin in the sun, and
rot like week-old milk.

Liz

Let us become new,
washed and cleansed.

Kenya

Daddy didn't make me who I am.
He made me who I am not.

Tammy

A beautiful flower,
breaking loose from its roots.

Alicia

A wild vine,
clinching the world into my palms.
Now breathing new life and love.

HALLELUJAH!
To God be the GLORY.
My Father breathed a new breath into me
and from the ashes,

In Unison

I rose.

The Phoenix

looking in the mirror,
I see love
in its purest form.
I feel His spirit gripping my skin and flowing freely
through my lungs.
I am here.

Selfish

I like to keep my stuff in order
can't nobody touch it but me.

I start to cringe when I see women give theirs away
to the next man they see.

Oh, no, I'm too selfish.
This is mine and its somewhere under
lock and key.

Deep down under an X, she purrs gently.

I want my things to be handled with care.
I'm fragile and will bruise
at the touch of rough hands.

Don't you know,
I'm made from the sands
of the purest gold?

My stuff has a history and I ain't never told a soul.

And eventually, one day,
I'll let these things go.
But for now, they all mine.

and like the blood diamonds, they shine.

Short &
(not so) Sweet

Breaking Chains

Sitting on the edge of her bed, Ife writes the last line to her poem: *I want out.* Hearing the footsteps of her boyfriend (whom she's been seeing for three years), she stuffs her journal underneath the mattress.

"Ife, where you at?" he calls from downstairs.

She answers, "I'm in the bedroom, Azizi."

Ife stands from the bed. Glancing in the mirror, she immediately loses herself in her own reflection. It isn't the same face she remembers from three years ago. She notices the darkness in her eyes and the paleness of her sable skin. This is a new Ife—a stranger.

"What are you doing in here by yourself?" he asks while standing in the doorway of their bedroom.

"What do you mean?"

Azizi moves behind his girlfriend and places his hand softly on her shoulder. It is cold. She flinches.

He speaks softly.

"Nia, Malik, and June are downstairs. We're about to practice some music. Don't you want to listen?"

"I'll come down."

"Alright."

He kisses her on her cheek and races back down the steps to join his band mates. Ife follows him down the stairs and sits in the living room, as the band begin its first number. She sways her head back and forth; the congas remind her of the summer vacations she used to take back home to Mozambique with her father. Remembrances of the hot African sun and gorgeous brown skin overwhelm her. She tilts her head back as the afternoon light, which creeps through the linen drapes, presses against her face. Her hair flows down her back like rivers. Malik plucks his kalimba lightly, Azizi strums his guitar and Nia and June sing a sweet folk song that reveals to Ife the reason why she's still with Azizi, but also why she is unhappy.

When they first started dating, both of them were fresh out of college and were looking for jobs. Ife worked at a small publishing company and Azizi had a government job with great benefits and salary. After dating for a while, Ife moved in with Azizi, and life was good until Azizi realized that he was miserable, and working a basic nine-to-five was becoming impossible. Azizi quit his job and started living off of the money that his band made from playing small gigs.

As a result, income in the house was extremely low and, from then on, a lot of the money came out of Ife's pockets. She was exhausted—physically exhausted from having to support a man whom she refused to marry under those conditions.

This was not the life that Ife had planned on living. Besides the lack of money, Ife was feeling a lack of love. Azizi's first love was music and that was clear in their relationship.

The music fades.

"You like that one Ife?" asks Nia.

"It was beautiful. It might even be my favorite," she says.

Azizi gleams with pride, while Ife stares out of the window aimlessly, watching the autumn leaves circle in the breeze like a game of "ring around the rosy." The band continues to play for the rest of the afternoon, and the emptiness that is hanging in Ife's spirit remains there until dawn.

■ ■ ■

Shadows play on the walls in the bedroom. In the darkness, Ife rests in Azizi's arms as if he is her only protection.

"Do you still love me, Azizi?"

"What? Of course I love you. Why would you ask me that?"

"Why do you love me?"

"Why? Because...you're everything that I imagined love to be."

"And what's that?"

"What's the matter? Why you keep asking me all these questions?"

"Because..." Ife peels off the tip of her half bitten fingernail. "I'm not happy."

"With what? Us?" Azizi asks.

"With any of this. Us. You. Me. You're never here anymore and I can't stand it. And we have no money; I'm always at my last dollar, and if I felt like there was still some type of love between us, I wouldn't even mind. But it's like everything in your life matters to you, except for me."

"You know that's not true. You do matter to me. It's just that my music is finally trying to get somewhere. I mean, I don't want you to have to spend your last dollar on toilet paper or food in the house. That's why I'm doing this. What I gotta do? Tell you I love you every day for you to get it?"

"That would be nice. Just a little reassurance would help."

"Jesus, Ife. After all these years, you've turned out to be one of *those* type of women."

Ife untangles herself from her boyfriend's arms.

"What?"

"You heard what I said, Ife. You're becoming one of those women who want me to drop everything that I'm doing just to be here with you. Your independence is one of the reasons why I fell in love with you in the first place."

She sits in shock. Her skin boils and her eyes water with anger.

"You've really got some nerve! I'm not begging you to stay home every day. Some of us actually *have* a job. All I'm saying is that you're always at some club doing God knows what, and I'm left here waiting for you to come home like your little puppy."

Ife catches her breath. "And then when you *are* home, you're just practicing all day. It's like I'm not even here."

"So what are you saying, Ife?"

"What am I saying? Baby, if you haven't heard anything that I just said then that's the issue right there!"

"Do you want to leave me?"

"That wasn't my first choice, but since you obviously have no intentions of making me stay then ...YES, I want to leave."

Her words frighten her, and she wants, so badly, to stuff them right back inside her mouth. She realizes that she's giving up the one person whom she thought she would be with forever. There was once a time when Azizi made her feel like she lived in a world filled with butterflies, afternoon kisses, and rose petals. But now she is giving up on what *she* knew to be love.

Azizi turns on the light.

"Well what are you waiting for? Go."

"Just like that, huh? You want me to just pack everything up and leave?"

"Ife, it's after midnight, you're jumping down my throat about how unhappy you are, and when I tell you to leave, you're still unhappy. Do you even know what you want?"

The room becomes uncomfortably quiet and the question rings in her head like the banging of a gong.

"I want..."

"You want what?"

"I just want my life back!"

"Exactly. You want *your* life back. All you think about is Ife. You don't care that I'm always out so that I can help you with money. You don't care about my passions. The only things you care about are your stupid books and journals. That's always been your problem since I've known you."

"Well maybe it is my problem. This whole situation is my problem. For the past few months, I've been wondering why I'm even here, Azizi. I don't love you like I used to. And don't sit there and tell me that you love me like you always have, because I know you don't. I can feel it."

Azizi palms his face as Ife stands from the bed and begins to pack a small bag of clothes.

"So maybe it is best that I go."

He watches Ife pack her things, and even though deep down in his heart he wants to stop her, he knows that there's no use in keeping an unhappy woman in his home.

Ife leaves the bedroom and runs down the stairs to the front door. Azizi follows her. She opens the door, and is half way out the house when Azizi grabs her hand. She snatches her hand back and continues to leave.

"Ife, just give me your hand!"

She pauses, but then walks a few steps back into the door way. Hesitatingly, she places her hand in Azizi's palm. He stares into her eyes, and although music dances through the grasp, the light that once shined in Ife's eyes is no longer there. The breeze blows ferociously, and Azizi loosens his grip from her hand, allowing Ife to walk away.

The door slams behind her, and instantly, Ife feels alone and lost in the city that she's been living in all of her life. Yet, with each step that she takes to her car, she feels all of her burdens and heartache peel, like dried glue, from her skin. She is free.

Sweet Nancy Kole

She was a tall vivacious woman that could always be seen with a cigarette. Funny thing about her was that she never smoked a day in her life. Secretly, she gagged at the smell, but our beloved would do just about anything to make it seem like she was dripping with sex appeal.

Her bronze hair bounced while she switched her big hips. Her lips curled, as she smiled at all the guys at the bar, and her eyes scorned every brown woman that envied her.

She wasn't just your average Baltimore woman. *She* was Nancy Kole. Sweet Nancy Kole that every man on the West side dreamed about at night while his wife was turned over sleeping. She was twenty nine years old, and had a five year old son who was somewhere lost in the system. She didn't even give him a name, yet she made sure that everyone knew hers; the last thing she wanted was to be forgotten.

There was something about Nancy that everyone seemed to love. Maybe it was the way she would light up a room or the sassy way she spoke. I'm not sure, but what I do know for certain is that she adored the attention.

Attention used to be an uncommon thing in her life, but when she found it, she held on to it tightly. Men wanted her badly, and with just a flash of a few big bills, Nancy was theirs for the night.

Unfortunately, and quite ironically, that same need for attention and love was what fiercely snatched her life away in a matter of seconds.

■ ■ ■

It was a hot summer night in East Baltimore. Like always, the clubs were jumping with ragtime; the streets were filled with drunks, high rollers, and prostitutes who you would have never known was one, because she was probably next to you, falling out, in church last Sunday morning.

Mobs of people stood out on the sidewalks and in the street; the bars were jam packed. So there they danced, intoxicatedly, as alcohol and melodic jazz splashed through their veins.

Nancy Kole sluggishly leaned against the side of Milly's Bar in a tight blouse that made her breasts appear bigger than they were. About fifteen people or so gathered around her. With a burning cigarette in her hand, she swayed her head from left to right, while she listened to the woman standing in front of her sing all types of riffs and runs. Sure, this lady was a good singer, but Nancy was much better and she knew it. She took a sip of her fourth drink and stood as straight as she could.

"Go ahead, Nancy! Show her what you can do," they screamed.

Nancy looked her opponent dead in the eye and began to scat to the faint snare playing inside of Milly's. The crowd jumped, cheered, and snapped their fingers to Nancy's tune, as her defeated opponent rolled her eyes and walked away. The cheering continued for awhile until Nancy's friend Honey broke up the circle to whisper something in her ear.

"Watcha doin', Honey? You messin' up my groove now."

"Nancy, some ole man came down here to see ya!"

"Oh shoot. What ole man? I ain't got no man! I'm just as free as I wanna be. Right, y'all?" Nancy spun in a dizzy circle and laughed with her admirers as Honey tugged on her arm.

"No, Nancy. I ain't say *your* ole man! Somebody wanna see you! You know, check you out! Now, go see what big daddy over there talkin' bout!"

Nancy fluffed the few curls that she had left in her hair and patted down her skirt, making sure it hugged her thighs the way she liked.

She stomped down the street in her five-inch heels to the dark gray Ford.

Nancy yelled out, "What's goin' on Daddy? You wanna check me out, eh? Well, Imma let you know now it's gonna cost ya. I ain't no cheap thrill!"

The older man, who sat in the driver's seat, slowly cracked his window and winked while sticking out two one hundred dollar bills. Nancy smirked, snatched the money, and stuck it in her bra. She caressed the roof of the car and glided to the other side to get in.

The Ford reeked with cigarette smoke, but Nancy didn't mind. She just stretched her body like a purring cat and loosened the mysterious man's tie, as he held onto her like she was the last woman on earth. He kissed her a thousand times.

"They told me you were the best in town," he slurred between kisses.

"*They* are right, baby."

"Yeah? I've been checkin' you out 'round here for the past couple weeks. I dig how you switch your hips and lick those soft lips of yours. Yeah, I see you do it all the time."

"You like what you see, hmm?"

"Yeah."

Beads of sweat formed on his forehead, when he kissed her again, but deeply this time. Nancy moaned just the way he wanted while his hands moved all over her thick body.

"Tell me you love me, baby," he whispered.

"Man, I love you just as much as you love me."

Disappointed with her answer, he demanded again. "Tell me you love me, baby!"

"Be quiet, man. You're just a lil' drunk. Be quiet," she whispered.

By this time, the windows were fogged and the temperature was insanely hot. Nancy giggled and continued to grind her hips on the stranger. Aggressively, he tilted her head back and then gripped her neck tightly. Nancy's body stiffened.

"Get off of me!"

He squeezed harder and harder until her olive skin became frighteningly pale. He shivered when she exhausted her last liquored breath.

Realizing what he had done, the crazy fool reached across Nancy's body and opened the door. A whirlpool of ragtime and laughter rushed inside the car, as he pushed the corpse onto the hard cement. He slammed the car door shut and sped off into the night, looking for the next woman that would tell him the words he had never once heard.

From the distance, Honey looked over and noticed that the car sped off. She smiled, assuming that Nancy went off with the high roller. But her smile soon disappeared when she saw a body curled against the curb. She jetted across the street.

"My God! Somebody come over here! Nancy's dead!"

But no one could hear her cries over all the jazz. Honey got up and ran back into the crowd in tears, pointing over to Nancy's body. They all ran over to Nancy and stood over her, sprinkling tears over her body like holy water, until an ambulance arrived.

The lights stayed on at Milly's that night, and once sweet Nancy's body was taken away, everyone stopped weeping, almost at once. And, together, they danced wildly beneath the streetlights.

Widow

a novella

I've never felt comfortable sitting in a circle. It's like there is nowhere for me to hide; I'm completely exposed.

"Lena, are you ready to share with us this evening?"

My heart races as I glance at Jasmine, the group therapy leader. Everyone in the room has shared except for me. I guess they wouldn't let me go a third week without saying anything. I don't want to, but they keep staring at me so I have no choice but to speak.

I bite down on my bottom lip so hard that I begin to taste a drop of blood on my tongue.

"Hi...my name is Lena Jones."

"Hi, Lena," all of the women say in unison. They sound like robots.

I exhale to calm my nerves. "I'm just now starting to sleep through the whole night." Don't cry, Lena. Do not cry.

"I get so lonely in that house...it's too big for just one person."

The woman next to me rubs her hand in a light circular motion on my back.

My head pounds, as all of the memories that I've ever shared with Darius come rushing to my mind like flooding waters.

"D-D-Dar-" I stop and start over. "My husband died. It's been just about, uh, two months...and I still haven't been able to accept it."

Everyone, especially Jasmine, is gazing at me as if I am a piece of art that's plastered on a gallery wall. She's got this strange look in her eyes and it makes me want to vanish right in front of her.

"How did your husband die?" someone whispered.

Like a reflex, my eyes shut tightly, trying to block the images of that evening. I wipe the tears that fall when I reopen them.

"I can still smell the food burning," I say with a shaky voice.

"I was cooking dinner when I heard the phone ring. I forgot that I had left the cordless in my bedroom, so, so I ran upstairs. When I answered the phone, there was a police officer on the other line."

I stop talking, but I can still hear the lingering echo of my voice. In the silence, I quickly scan all of the sympathizing faces. These women are looking at me almost as if they know me. Perhaps they do.

Someone passes me a tissue.

"Would you like to stop there?" Jasmine asks while I pat beneath my eyes.

I nod my head and look down at the hardwood floor.

"Thank you for sharing, Lena," everyone says.

"Sharing will get easier each time you decide to open up to us," Jasmine says.

She looks around the room. Some women are crying while a few others look spaced out, trapped in their own minds.

"I know that I say this all of the time, but I want everyone in here to know that grieving is not something that you have to do alone. When you come in here, feel free to cry and to be in pain. We are here to help and listen to each other. Don't feel as if you have to hold anything back," she says.

Some people nod as she speaks.

"Well, I think that we can end on that note and continue next week," she says.

At once, all of the women stand and the room grows loud as they mingle with one another. This would be an ideal time for me to make friends, but instead I find my way straight to the door. As I squeeze through a couple of social circles, a few women look at me strangely when I walk past them. I'm just a few steps from the door, and I feel like I'm about to cross the finish line. But just as my hand touches the doorknob, I hear my name.

"Lena, wait a second!" Jasmine says.

I drop my head.

As soon as I turn around, there she is. Jasmine is a sweet young lady with a big smile. Her complexion is slightly lighter than mine, and her hair is styled in a low natural haircut that I haven't seen sisters wear since I was a kid. It looks great on her. I don't think I could ever cut all of my hair.

"Thanks again for participating," she says, looking up at me.

For such a petite woman she has a lot of presence, yet her long flowing skirt makes her look a lot shorter. Since I've been coming here, she's dressed in loose and colorful clothing. And today is no exception. Complimenting her burnt orange skirt, she wore a purple camisole with a long and worn blue cardigan. She has a bohemian vibe to her that I kind of like.

I don't respond to her comment, so she clears her throat.

"Listen, seeing as this is still a hard thing for you to cope with, I want to give you my number. I like for everyone to be able to talk to me if they need to, so please feel free to call me at anytime."

The gold bangles that she's wearing on her wrist chime, as she hands me a small piece of paper with her number on it. I grip it in my hand.

"Thanks, but I really have to go."

"Of course."

She hugs me tightly. My body tenses; it is the first time I have been hugged since Darius has passed. I let go and turn for the door.

"See you next week," she says.

As soon as the door opens, the wind pushes past me. Opening my hand, I watch the little piece of paper fly down the street. I shrug and quickly button my jacket while walking down Charles Street towards my car.

The scent of lavender trails beneath my nose, as the candle burns on my desk. I sit, palming my face, while staring at an intimidating stack of bills. Eventually, I get the strength to go through each of them, one by one. Water, electricity, cable… these are the type of things that Darius always handled and insisted that I not worry myself with.

"I bring home the money, so I'll pay the bills," he'd say.

Well, I guess this is my job now.

"If it weren't for this insurance money, I don't know how all of this would get paid off," I say while tearing blank checks out of my checkbook.

I sit for a while, looking around my room. I realize that this space is a constant reminder of Darius.

His belongings are intact just like he left them. Some of his papers are still here on this desk and his shirts are still folded in the top right dresser drawer. I haven't the strength to throw his things out because I don't want to admit it to myself that he is gone. Strangely, I have imagined that one day he'll walk into this house and say, "Baby, I'm home." But I know it's time for me to do it.

I get up from the desk and walk over to what used to be *our* bed. Am I really about to do this? I sit on the edge of the bed and look towards the window. The last of the day's sun fades through the thin curtains. I take a deep breath and find the nerve to start the task that I've been avoiding for months. Looking around the room, I notice that my husband has more things than I do. I grab a large trash bag, and I begin with his shoes. Pair by pair, I throw them each inside the bag except for his favorite black loafers. I slip my tiny feet into them and snigger as I realize that I look like a child trying to fill her father's shoes. My laughing surprises me.

Next are his pants. I remove my own and step into his, before dumping the rest into the bag. Opening the closet door, I try on one of Darius's shirts. Smelling his faint fragrance that was left on the collar, I nearly melt. I softly kiss the inside of it and then I take the rest of the shirts off of the hangers to throw them into the trash bag as well. Lastly, I come across his beloved ties, and immediately I put his favorite blue one around my neck. Looking in the long mirror, I try my best to visualize him, but I can only see my miserable self—a poor replica.

I close my eyes and imagine that Darius is here, holding me closely and reminding me that everything will be okay. With my arms wrapped around myself, I reopen my eyes to reality. This is the first moment where his absence seems completely real. Looking down at my left hand, my wedding band still shimmers just as it did when he first slid it on my finger. I gently slide off the ring and place it at the bottom of my jewelry box. Forcing myself to accept my reality, I change back into my clothes.

Just as I sit back at the desk, the telephone rings, but I don't see the point in answering it. So I let it ring and ring until my answering machine comes on.

"Hi, Lena. This is Jasmine from group therapy. I had your number on file and I was just calling to see if all is well. I noticed you weren't at the last three sessions and you never called me."

I begin to write out a check, while I listen to the message.

"I really would like to talk with you more, so if you could give me a call that would be awesome! My number is 410-941-5555. Talk to you soon."

She hangs up and I groan.

What gives her the right to call me? Shouldn't that be against the rules or something?

That place wasn't for me. I don't like the idea of having to sit amongst a group of women who are just as sad and pathetic as I am. How are they supposed to help me if they are sitting around crying too? Why should I have to share my most intimate secrets and thoughts to a group of complete strangers? I'd rather just deal with all of this myself. It's what I've been doing for the past two months anyway.

Something dragged me back to this place. Darius and I loved this restaurant and I never thought I'd find myself back here. I ask for the table in the corner, not so that no one will notice that I'm alone, but so that my loneliness will not be apparent.

"Hi Mrs. Jones! Long time no see," says my waitress.

Her name slips my mind.

"Hi. How are you?"

"Pretty good. Where's Mr. Jones? Out trying to find a parking space?"

"No. It's just me."

A confused look appears on her face, but I think she senses my discomfort so she changes the subject.

"Well, what can I get you this evening?"

"I'll try the beef stew."

"Haha. Mr. Jones' favorite. He finally made you try it huh?"

"Yeah...I guess so."

"Great. I'll put your order in right away," she says while walking swiftly from my table.

I feel like I want to cry but I know that there's no use. While waiting for my food, I look around, watching the other people in the restaurant. Everyone seems happy, like they have no care in the world. What I would give to be in their shoes.

Time passes, and the waitress brings me my beef stew. I lay a napkin over my skirt and I inhale deeply over the stew just like Darius would do. It smells so good and eventually I realize that it tastes even better.

As I eat, I do not allow myself to think of Darius. I want to be completely alone and far away from my thoughts. For some moments, I am lost in my meditation until I hear a roar of laughter coming from the party that's sitting just a few tables away from me. They are laughing hard and I watch them as they wipe the tears from their eyes.

I am about to turn back to my stew, but something catches my eye outside of the window behind the laughing table. There's a man standing there, and it looks as if he's smiling at me. I squint, trying to make out the thin figure. My heart nearly stops when he blows a kiss at me. I glimpse over my shoulder to see if maybe he's looking at someone else, but the ladies behind me are too enthralled in their conversation to even notice him.

Who am I fooling? I know exactly who he is, and he knows it's me. I stare at him just a little longer. This can't be.

"How are you doing over here, Mrs. Jones?" my waitress asks.

I jump.

" I'm sorry. I didn't mean to—"

"It's okay," I say, discreetly looking out of the window behind her.

"How's the stew?" she asks.

"Delicious," I say. "Everything is just fine."

"OK. Let me know if you need anything," she says while walking away.

When she leaves, the man who could not have been anyone else but Darius is gone. I shake my head at the thought of something so ridiculous. Embarrassed at myself, I look down and begin to eat again.

Bringing the spoon up to my mouth, I feel a gentle stroke on my left hand. Startled, I look up from the stew.

"Hi, baby."

I release my hand from his and use it to cover my mouth.

"It's OK," he says.

I look around the room to see if anyone is paying attention to us, but no one is.

"Darius…how? What are you doing here?"

"I had to see you."

My voice is a light whisper. I place my hand back down to hold his. It still feels like smooth silk. I've missed this feeling.

"Are you here forever?"

He shakes his head no.

"Why? Why not!"

"Because, Lena. I just can't."

My voice is shaky. "Why did you leave, Darius?"

He leans in and places his finger on my lips.

"You look beautiful," he says.

I touch his face and he smiles.

"I've been miserable," I say.

"I'm so sorry."

"All I do is lay around thinking about you."

"I'm always thinking of you, Lena," he says.

"Do you hear me when I'm thinking of you?" I ask.

"No…"

I bite my lip nervously.

"The house looks a mess," I say, giggling. "I haven't had the urge to clean it in days."

"Well that's nothing new," he says.

"Oh be quiet!"

He pushes a piece of my hair behind my ear. "I miss this face," he says.

"Just stay here. Let's just go back to our normal lives!"

I feel a few tears hiding in the corners of my eyes.

"Lena, it doesn't work like that."

"What do you mean?"

He shakes his head.

"Then let me go with you! Please, Darius."

"Lena, stop. You have to be strong. I need you to be strong for the both of us."

"I can't."

"Yes, you can. Just remember that I love you and I haven't stopped loving you."

He leans in closer to kiss me.

"Excuse me, can I borrow this chair?"

Still holding the spoon in my mouth, I look up at the man standing next to my table and then back down at the empty chair across from me.

"Yeah…sure."

"Thanks," he says pulling the chair away. Pulling Darius away.

■ ■ ■

I take off my jacket and place my keys on the counter. My heart hasn't stopped racing since I left the restaurant. I don't know what happened tonight, but I need to tell somebody before I drive myself crazy. I always feel Darius with me. Sometimes I can even hear his laugh or old things that he might have said, but this was different. I *saw* him. I talked with him…at least I thought I did. I'm not sure if this is normal or if I've completely hit rock bottom.

I walk over to my answering machine and replay the message from Jasmine, so that I can retrieve her phone number. When she says it, I save it into my cell phone. As much as I hate to do it, I'm going to call her first thing in the morning.

I am growing too big for my clothes. This hideous blouse is one of the few shirts I have that still fits me, so I have to wear it.

After squeezing into a pair of jeans, I sit at the vanity table to brush my hair back into its usual long ponytail and I braid it just like Darius always loved for me to wear it.

Next, I put just a little foundation on my face and a few strokes of blush on my cheeks. Hopefully when I meet with Jasmine today, she won't notice these bags below my eyes or this bad break out of bumps on my face.

I take a deep breath and stand in front of the mirror, forced to ask myself the question "How do I look?"

If I were in the mood to be honest with myself, I'd say I look awful. So I lie.

"You look great, girl."

The last thing I want is for Jasmine to look at me and know off the bat that I've been going through it.

When I finally feel comfortable with my appearance, I leave my house and head to Druid Hill Park where Jasmine asked that I meet her.

In the car, the self-help CD that I saw being displayed on the check out counter at the drug store is playing.

"I am in charge of my own destiny," says the narrator.

I repeat after him. "I am in charge of my own destiny."

"I have a purpose, and I am in search of this purpose."

"I have a purpose, and I-" I suck my teeth, eject the CD and fling it to the backseat.

I'd rather drive in silence.

Arriving at the park, I drive around a few times before actually parking. Something inside of me is telling me to go back home, but the other part of me knows that this has become my last resort.

I find a parking space close by. After I turn off my car, I continue to sit, gripping the steering wheel. My heart is pacing and butterflies are flying madly in the pit of my stomach.

"I am in charge of my own destiny." I take a breath. "I am in charge of my own destiny," I repeat.

I close my eyes, thinking back to a few days ago when I imagined Darius. He was so beautiful. Just seeing him gave me the strength to even drive here today. I replay our conversation in my head, wishing that I could have kissed him and held him close to my heart. I sigh and reopen my eyes, before getting out of the car.

It is one of the warmer days in March, and probably the most beautiful day Baltimore has seen in a while. I stand looking at the bright green manicured lawn and the grassy hills in the distance. The trees are beginning to fill up with pink and purple buds.

Walking through the grass, I spot Jasmine. She's sitting with an older woman. I stop where I am and stand far away enough so that she won't notice that I'm near by.

I stare at the two of them, as they get up from the bench. They hug each other and the woman walks away. Jasmine sits back down, glances at her watch, and then looks around for a bit. She's waiting for me, but I continue to stand in the distance, juggling the idea of walking towards her or running back to my car.

"You need to talk to someone," I say to myself.

I take another deep breath and begin to make my way over to her. She sees me and waves. She resembles someone of royalty, waving to her people. I hope that one day I'll look as radiant as she does.

"I'm glad you made it!" she says.

I smile softly.

"Oh, don't be shy. Have a seat."

We sit at the same time.

"I'm so glad you called me," she says.

"I should be the one thanking you. Why did you call me anyway?"

"Well because I could sense that you really needed help grieving," she says.

"You could sense that? How?"

"I've been counseling women who've been going through the same thing as you for some time now. Even I had to overcome a lot in my life. So when I saw how emotional you were getting while sharing with us, I could tell that you were having a hard time letting it all out."

I am quiet.

"Am I right?"

I nod my head. "That was the first time I had even began to tell the story to anyone."

"You never told anyone? What about your family?"

I grunt. "What family?"

"Where's your family?" This time she looks more concerned.

I shake my head and Jasmine sighs. "What made you try group therapy?"

"I was tired of being sad and feeling sorry about myself, so I went on-line and I started looking for ways to deal with grief, and a lot of the search results said to seek counseling or to attend group therapy sessions."

"It's great that you decided to get this kind of help," she says.

I try to fake a smile.

"Tell me a little about your husband."

A genuine smile creeps upon my face as I begin to think of him.

"He was a busy man…always in a rush."

"Yeah?"

"He was a city council rep for the eighth district."

"Ah a politician…the eighth district?"

"Yeah that covers communities from Edmondson Village to Beech-field."

"Tough areas."

"Which is why he was so busy… there was so much he wanted to do to help his city."

"That's great. I love to see good politicians actually keeping up their side of the bargain."

"It was. He made it so that cameras and lights were put up on street corners, schools were fixed up and officers were out and about in the heavy drug areas."

"Wow. I bet he spent a lot of time away from home, huh?"

"Yeah…he did. But it wasn't a problem. He had to be away if he wanted to make a difference. I didn't mind. I just made sure he had a warm plate waiting for him when he got back."

Jasmine scrunches her lips. "Hmm"

The wind picks up, blowing my hair wildly. I push a few pieces behind my ear.

"How did it feel being the wife of a big time politician?"

I stop and think. "I don't know. I guess it was okay… it was stressful at times though."

"Really? How so?"

"Because I was the First Lady, if you will. Everyone expected me to be just as good as my husband. I had to make sure I looked good at all times. My image was just as important as his."

Jasmine nodded with a look of empathy.

"In the group session, you began to tell us how he passed. Do you think that you can finish the story now?"

I nod my head yes. "It was a car accident."

"I'm sorry," she says while rubbing my knee.

"Another one of those late evenings…he was on his way home from the office and was hit by a drunk driver…just a few blocks away from the house."

"That's terrible."

"I didn't know what to do with myself. There was no one here to help me, no one to tell… All I had was myself. Can you imagine how that feels?"

"I know exactly how that feels," she says.

A few loud screams and laughter are in the distance, so I look away to see where the sounds are coming from. I smile as soon as I see that there are children running and playing on the playground.

"You don't have any children do you?"

"No. Darius didn't want any," I say turning back to Jasmine.

"Did you?"

"I wanted Darius to be happy."

"But did you want to have children?"

I glance at the children once again.

"I don't know."

Jasmine watches the children for a while longer. At first she smiles, but the more she stares at them, the sadder she begins to look.

"Are you okay?" I ask, but she ignores me.

"Lena, how important was Darius's happiness to you?"

"All I wanted was for my husband to feel like he married the greatest woman in the world. I gave him my all. And if he wasn't happy, I wasn't happy.

She looks into my eyes. It scares me because no one has ever looked at me like this before.

"What?" I ask.

"You just remind me so much of myself…I used to be you. I did everything for my husband…of course, I had no choice, but I did it."

"What do you mean you had no choice?"

"I was in an abusive marriage. Married at 18 and divorced by 25."

I nod, wanting her to keep talking. It wouldn't be fair if I was the only one who had to pour out my guts to a complete stranger.

"I was that young girl that you hear about everyday, completely in love with the wrong man. Everyone warned me about him, but being so naive I paid them no mind…and in consequence I found myself crying every single night, waking up with new cuts and bruises."

I lowered my head, feeling sorry for her. You would have never known that she had been through so much just by looking at her. She looked nearly perfect. All of this time I had thought she was just some happy go lucky tree hugger that wanted to change the world one person at a time.

"I lost myself in that relationship, and I think that's the same thing that happened to you."

I look up at her.

"That I lost myself?"

"Yes." Jasmine pauses, struggling to find the words to create an explanation. "Eh... how do you feel about your hair right now?"

I grip my long braided ponytail, and it slaps my back when I let go. "It's okay, I guess. I always wear it this way."

"Why? Why have you always worn it that way?"

"Because Dar-" I stop myself.

"Go ahead...say it. Because Darius liked it that way, right? You hate your hair in that style don't you?"

"Not really, I just-"

"Don't you?"

"It could be better," I say in nearly a whisper.

"So why don't you change it? What's stopping you?"

"What's the point? There's no one to impress now."

"Yes, there is."

"Who? I don't plan on seeing someone else anytime soon."

"You, Lena! You. Try impressing yourself. Make yourself feel loved and welcomed. I'm truly sorry that your husband passed, but you've put Darius over your own needs and wants. And now you have to change that."

"How do I do that?"

"Work on you. Do things that you've always wanted to do, but never did. Think about the foods you wanted to eat, the places you've always wanted to travel to. Take your mind off of Darius for a while."

I fold my arms. I don't care if she's right or not. Who is she to tell me not to think about my husband? So what if I pampered him and did everything with his best interest in mind? That's what I was always told a wife was supposed to do. Now, I'm in the wrong?

I grab my purse and put it over my shoulder.

"I'm sorry, but I don't think this is a good idea, Jasmine."

"Why because I'm telling you something that you don't want to hear? You can't just up and run from the truth every time you hear it, Lena."

"You don't know me, okay. I'm not like you or any of the other women you've talked to before."

"But you are! And you're hurting just like we are. If you run away from the truth, you'll never get better."

"I guess I'll just have to take that risk," I say walking back to my car.

I miss him in the mornings. Especially times like these when I'm trying to cook breakfast. I stretch my arm to the top cabinet for the sugar but I cannot reach it. I begin to call out Darius's name for help, but I stop myself. I take a deep breath and grab the stool from the laundry room to stand on.

"One day at a time," I say quietly.

After pouring a few teaspoons of sugar in my grits, I sit alone to eat at the kitchen table.

I've been jittery all morning and I cannot stop thinking about how rude I was to Jasmine. I didn't mean to walk out on her like I did. When I finish eating, I swipe my keys from off of the kitchen counter and I drive to the center where the Jasmine works. I want to apologize, and hopefully she'll agree to try again.

As I walk through the door, I notice the receptionist is looking over her glasses, staring at me.

"Can I help you?"

"Hi. I'm looking for Jasmine uh…she facilitates the group therapy sessions."

"Just a moment," she says.

I watch as she picks up the phone and dials a four-digit extension number.

She forces a smile as the phone rings.

"Jasmine, someone is here to speak with you…I'm not sure…"

"Do you have an appointment?" she asks me.

"I don't."

"No, she doesn't."

The receptionist nods her head and hangs up the phone.

"You can wait outside her office. It's just down the hall," she says.

I walk down the hallway. It's long and dark and I feel like I'm at some sort of psychiatric ward. The hall seems never ending, until I see a closed door. I peak through the window and notice that Jasmine is talking with someone. I think she sees me so I quickly take a step back. A few minutes later she opens the door to let out her client. She takes a look at me.

"Lena, what a surprise." She motions for me to come inside.

Jasmine's office is very bright and vibrant, almost like a Pre-K classroom. It almost scares me when I realize how organized everything is; there isn't one thing out of place. As I sit down in the chair that's in front of her desk, I notice that she only has one picture displayed and even that is slightly turned, making it hard for me to see what or who it is. It looks like it could be of a baby. Maybe a niece or a nephew.

She slouches in her chair. "So what brings you here? I figured you were done with therapy after yesterday."

"I'm sorry. I didn't mean for that to happen."

"But you did mean to leave," she said.

"No, I'm serious. I was just nervous about the whole thing…and like you said, I wasn't ready to hear the truth."

"It's okay. You're not the first person to storm out of the room during a session."

I stare at her pen as she repetitively taps it on the desk.

"So what now? Do you want to start over?" she asks.

"Please?"

Jasmine agrees to see me, and she wastes no time in picking up right where she left off yesterday. I try my best to listen with an open mind, because whether I liked it or not, she was right and I needed the help. For nearly a half hour we do an exercise where Jasmine asks me about the type of food I eat, the clothes I wear, the music I listen to etc. A lot of my answers are Darius's favorites. I never realized how much he has taken out of me. I am happy when we finish.

"We can do this once a week if you want," she says.

"I think I'd like that," I say, standing from my seat.

"One last thing," she says. "I really think you need to get in touch with some of your family or friends. You need to talk to other people…people who you really know and trust."

"Jasmine, I don't know if I can do that"

"What do you mean?"

"I haven't talked to my parents in years. I can't just call them out of the blue."

"Why can't you? Stop putting limitations on yourself!"

"You don't understand. I said so many hurtful things to my parents that I wouldn't be surprised if they've completely erased me from their lives."

"What did you say?"

I sit back down. Jasmine waits for me to speak.

"Well, I'm originally from California. I went to college at California State University in Los Angeles. That's where I met Darius. We dated from our sophomore to senior year and when it was time for us to graduate, I planned to stay home in California, but Darius wanted me to go back home with him to Baltimore.

"I knew nothing about Baltimore or any city on the east coast for that matter. But because I was so in love, I decided that it wasn't such a bad idea. Around this time my parents were constantly nagging me and like every twenty one year-old, I wanted my own space and freedom.

"When I told my parents about my decision, of course they were against the whole idea, which lead to a conversation that escalated into a huge argument."

"Well what was the argument?"

I shake my head in embarrassment. "I told them both how much I hated them and how I hated living with them because they never supported anything I wanted to do with my life. I also told them that they no longer had a daughter and to plan to never see my face again. So after the fight, I stayed at Darius' apartment for a few weeks until it was time for us to board the plane.

"I haven't talked to them since…that was ten years ago."

"Hmm. Well I'm telling you the only way you'll get through to them now is if you just pick up the phone and call them. But it's up to you."

6

I've never felt so intimidated by a rack of clothes. I decided to get up early and come to the mall, seeing as though I'm too big for most of my clothes, and for the simple fact that it's been a while since I bought something for myself. Every time I bought something, it was usually for Darius.

I almost feel awkward as I pick through a rack of dresses. None of these dresses are anything that I would normally wear. As a matter of fact, Darius would probably make me return one of these back to the store if I were to bring it home.

"Where do you think you're going with that on?" he'd ask. "The whole city will be talking if they see you in that."

I laugh to myself. He could be so uptight at times, and I guess that's why I can be such a stick in the mud now.

As I continue to browse through the dresses, a bright yellow sun dress catches my eye. I take the dress off of the rack and hold it up in front of me.

"This looks different," I say.

I place the dress back on the rack and keep looking.

"Oh just try it on," I think.

It won't hurt if I do. Quickly, I take the dress off the rack and head to the dressing room. When I get inside, I peel off my jeans and baggy tee shirt. I stand nearly naked in front of the mirror. I move in so close to the mirror that I feel the cool glass pressed against my stomach. I take a good look at my eyes, trying to see if the real me is hiding deep down inside them. I can't see her.

Taking a step back from the mirror, I place each foot inside the sun dress and pull it up. My face glows just as bright as the dress does, when I see how beautiful it looks on me. Touching my bare shoulders, I turn to the side to see my uncovered back. It looks strong. No more hiding this pretty brown skin. I undo my braid and shake my hair as I pull off the ponytail holder. My hair tickles my back. I giggle as I stand on my tippy toes, letting the bottom of my dress flow beneath my feet. I look good. Covering my mouth, I hold back the loud screech of joy that's bursting inside of me.

■ ■ ■

I always wanted a group of girlfriends like this. Wearing a light sweater over my new yellow sun dress, I'm sitting in a cozy love seat in Jasmine's living room, listening to her and her two best friends, Melanie and Kristin, reminisce about their "good days." Their laughs echoed throughout the house. I'm happy she invited me over. I needed to get out of the house. Jasmine has the radio playing low on an "oldies but goodies" station. I hear *My Endless Love* playing faintly and I try to ignore the fact that it was our song.

As they talked and laughed, I eyed Jasmine's home. The living room alone is filled with African artifacts and antiques. Strong fragrances of incense creep through the room. It is quite different from her office. Not as bright. Next to her stereo, there is a tall bookcase filled with black literature, psychology and counseling books.

"Oh I'm sorry, Lena. I know you have no idea what we're talking about," Jasmine says.

"No, no. It's fine."

The women stop laughing and change the subject.

"So what do you do for a living, Lena?" Melanie asks.

I sip the last of my iced tea and clear my throat before answering.

"Well, I actually don't work."

"Oh, she has a man that brings in all the bread. Must be nice," Kristin says jokingly.

Jasmine glances at me, anticipating my response.

I smile. "No. Actually I was a housewife, but my husband just passed not too long ago, so I haven't gotten a job since."

Melanie's smile erases from her face.

"I'm so sorry," Kristin said.

"Don't worry about it. You didn't know."

"I know it's been hard for you," Melanie says.

"Yes. But I have some good days as well bad ones."

"I'm sure Lena doesn't want to talk about this," Jasmine says.

"You're right. I'm sorry," Melanie says.

I grow quiet, realizing how awkward this moment has just become.

Jasmine grabs our empty cups and rinses them out in the kitchen sink. I head for the bathroom.

When I get to the top of the stairs, there's a door that's cracked open, allowing me to see a little inside. There are bright blue walls, much different from all of the beige ones in the house. I want to go inside, but I continue to walk to the bathroom instead.

Back downstairs, Anita Baker's voice drips slowly like honey from the speakers.

"Whew girl, this is my song!" Jasmine says while walking into the living room.

I sit back in my seat and watch her as she moves in circles and sings at the top of her lungs.

"Go 'head, girl!" her friends say.

She really can't sing that well, but her passion distracts me from the sound. Kristin, Melanie and I begin to laugh hysterically as she walks over to me singing, *Same Ole Love*. She holds out her hand for me to join her. Still laughing, I shake my head no.

"Oh c'mon," she begs.

"I don't sing!"

"Neither do I!" She pulls me from off the couch and holds my hands as she turns in circles, continuing to perform.

I mumble the words to the song to satisfy her.

"I can't hear you!" she says while laughing.

I sing louder.

"There you go."

Before I know it, I'm spinning around like one of the Supremes, singing my heart out. By this time, Kristin and Melanie have joined us. As each note flies out of my mouth, I grow happier and happier. It was like I was in a Disney movie, being lifted in the air by hundreds of chirping birds. I don't recall ever feeling like this.

Jasmine stops dancing and turns to me with a look of astonishment.

"You sound amazing!"

She's embarrassing me. I've never sung like this in front of anyone.

"Thank you," I say nearly blushing.

She turns around and goes back to singing and dancing with the girls. I follow her lead.

"Cut it all off," I say to my hair stylist.

"Are you sure? All of this long, pretty hair!"

"Yes. I've never been more sure in my life."

"Alright then," she says, playing with a pair of scissors.

She spins me around in the chair and my heart drops as I feel my long braid being cut. I look to the floor, watching the rest of my hair fall on the ground with every snip. When she's done, she spins me back around so that I can face the mirror. As soon as I see my reflection, I fall in love.

My stylist laughs at me. "Girl, you staring in that mirror hard ain't you?"

She doesn't know that this is the first time that I've ever truly appreciated what I saw in the mirror. It's almost like I'm seeing myself for the first time. I like the way my face looks without my hair always getting in the way. It looks free.

"It's beautiful," I say.

"I'm glad you like it," she says. "Why did you want to cut it all off anyway?"

I look at my long locks on the floor, and then back at the mirror.

"I just wanted it off of me. It was weighing me down…always in the way."

"It's funny how we give our hair so much power even when we aren't thinking about it," my stylist says.

I'm confused.

"I mean, you know, we spend hours in the mirror trying to fix it, and we spend so much money to get it done only for it to go unnoticed. We use it for compliments…as a cover up."

"Wow. That's the last thing I would've expected a hair stylist to say," I say jokingly.

She laughs. "Girl, I've been through it all. Short hair, curly hair, weaves, wigs. I mean everything. So I know exactly what you mean." She pats my back.

We smile at each other, and without an exchange of words, she's assured me that I'm not alone.

I slip her a twenty-dollar bill and I grin all the way out the door to my car.

Next stop is Jasmine's house.

Jasmine and I have decided to alternate having dinner at each other's home for the week. After I told her that contacting my parents was completely out of the question, she has taken me under her wing. We've grown into really good friends and I'm happy to have her around.

When I arrive at her house, I knock on the door a few times before she lets me in.

"Hi!" she says.

I smell alcohol on her breath. She told me that she doesn't drink.

"It isn't good for recovering women to drink, smoke...none of that," she once said.

"Hey," I say, walking through the door. "How are you?"

"Great! How are—Oh my God! You cut your hair!" She stumbles over to me, and touches the coils on my head.

"Yeah...are you sure you're alright?" I say as I watch her trip around.

"Don't I look alright?" She flops down on her couch.

I walk in the kitchen and the stove burner is a bright red, yet there's no food in sight. I turn the stove off and look back at her. In the corner of my eye, I can see that there's a wine bottle on the counter.

"Have you been drinking, Jasmine?"

"No."

"Jasmine..."

"Okay, fine. Maybe I had a little glass of wine. No big deal." She points her leg in the air as if she's a ballerina.

"Jasmine, this bottle is nearly empty! What have you been doing in here?"

"Drinking!"

I pour her a glass of water. " How about you drink this."

She snatches the glass from me, and the water splashes on her shirt. She shrieks.

"Drink it," I say.

I watch as she takes three big gulps. She lies back down on the couch and I sit next to her. Her eyes are barely open.

"I'm so glad you're here, Lena." Her words are crashing into each other.

"What happened?"

"I miss my baby," she sobs.

"What are you talking about?"

Her eyes stay closed, and I nudge her.

"Jasmine, What's going on?"

"It's his birthday," she says loudly.

"Who?"

She turns on her side "Christopher… he would've been ten today."

I have no idea who she is talking about. "Who is-" then I remember the photo of the baby on her desk. That must've been him.

"Jasmine, sit up and talk to me." I help her sit up straight. "Was he your son?" I ask softly.

She starts crying. "He was only three!"

I wipe a tear from my eye. "What happened to him?"

She gets up from the couch and stumbles over to the counter where the bottle of wine is. "He pushed him down the steps!"

She slams her glass on the counter and pours the remainder of the wine into it.

"I hope he rots in Hell!" she screams.

I watch her as she drinks until the glass is empty. I walk over to her and hug her tightly.

"It's alright," I say.

"It's not alright! I was supposed to fall! Not Christopher!" I feel her tears seeping through the cotton of my shirt.

"He had been beating me, on and off, for nearly an hour! And I was hurting, Lena! I wanted him to stop! I didn't want my son to see that happening to his mother. So I ran out of our bedroom. And I- I don't know how Christopher even got there, but he must've ran behind me…"

She pushes away from me.

"I was…I was standing in front of the steps, trying to back away from that crazy bastard … but he pushed me so hard!"

She turns her back to me, and stands still.

"I felt him behind me…but before I even realized what was happening, he had already fell and all I could hear was him screaming and those loud thumping sounds as he went down those steps," she says while pressing her hands over her ears.

I cover my mouth, feeling my tears run over my hands.

"Why didn't I fall instead?"

Paralyzed, I stand there crying. I have no idea how she feels. I thought I was the only one going through Hell, but she's got it worse. Without a second thought, I walk beside her and get down on my knees. I look up at her trembling body, and then I tug her hand. She gets down on her knees next to me, and I clasp her hands while she closes her eyes. I lower my head and begin to pray a prayer that my mother used to say with me every night before I went to sleep.

"God, grant me the serenity to accept the things I cannot change, courage to change the things that I can, and wisdom to know the difference."

■ ■ ■

The next morning, I wake up on Jasmine's couch. She's in the kitchen making coffee.

"Good morning," I mumble.

"Good morning," she says.

I sit up on the couch and rub my eyes, while Jasmine brings the coffee over to me.

"Here." She sits down on the ottoman. "I'm really sorry about last night."

"It's alright."

"I'm glad you were here. I'm not sure what I would've done to myself."

I take a sip of coffee. "Why didn't you tell me that you had a son before?"

"Everyone has their secrets, right?"

I shake my head. "No. You pretty much know all of mine."

"Well now you know all of mine… I don't know what happened. I thought I was over it, but his birthday just snuck up on me…and it hit me all over again."

"Like you told me, healing takes time. You can't just be over it."

"I know…I know."

I hug her again.

"Listen," she says, pulling away from me. "Can this just be between me and you?"

"Of course."

"Then I probably should show you."

Before I can question her, she heads for the steps and begins to walk upstairs. I follow behind her.

She opens the door to the room located right by the steps; it was the same room that I had noticed before. When I walked inside, the blue walls and light blue carpet greeted me.

"I made this room just for him," Jasmine says.

I walk around, looking at the many photographs of him that lined the walls. He was so handsome.

"What was he like?"

She holds a picture of him.

"He was the happiest little boy I've ever seen."

A big smile forms on my face.

"He loved to laugh and run around the house. He acted as if the world was his."

"He sounds so sweet."

"He was. He was my little angel."

We both sit on the floor and feel Christopher's spirit in the room. Jasmine breaks our silence.

"I don't know how much longer I'm going to be doing this whole counseling job," she says.

"What do you mean? You have to."

"How can I help someone else, when I'm not even all together?"

I am quiet.

"Plus there's so much more that I want do. I started doing this because I knew what it felt like to grieve and to hurt, and I wanted to help people who were having the same problem. But now it's draining me."

"Is it because of me?"

"You? No, of course not. Lena, you're different. You're the only person who has become my friend since I started this whole thing. And I mean a true friend."

I smile. "I feel like this is what I'm supposed to be saying to you."

"I guess I beat you to it." She pauses. "But what I'm saying is that I've never dreamed of actually counseling people and facilitating therapy sessions."

"Maybe this is what God sent you here to do. Maybe this is your calling...you just had to go through Hell to realize it."

"Maybe you're right," she says. " I don't know. I have to think about it."

"Just do what your heart tells you to do. I may be wrong."

She nods and then bursts into laughter.

"When did you become my therapist?"

I laugh to myself. When did I?

"I'm not the same girl that I was when I met you," I say, kneeling in front of Darius's grave.

Jasmine offered to come along with me, but this was a trip that I needed to take alone. For days, I've been writing poems and journal entries with things that I've wanted to tell Darius. Things that I wished I could tell him face to face. I haven't been to his grave site since the day I saw them drop him deep below the ground, and I said to myself that I wouldn't be back. But something inside of me told me to come here. It was a lingering feeling that told me to sit right here and talk to Darius because he'd be listening.

I take a deep breath, inhaling the morning.

"Darius, I…I came here to say thank you."

The birds are chirping loudly, and I stop and listen for a moment.

"Thank you for loving me, even though I was weak. I loved you because you were strong, and I secretly envied that about you. I longed for that same respect that you received."

I reach inside my bag and pull out a long stemmed rose. I flinch as its thorn pricks my finger.

"But since you've been gone, I've learned that I've had that respect all along. It was just hiding…deep down in here," I say, pointing to my heart.

"I'm stronger than I was on that last morning I saw you. You remember? I was nearly in tears because you ate your breakfast in one swallow, ran around the house mumbling the words of your speech, all while looking for your favorite tie, and not once did you stop to say "thank you." Not once did you even acknowledge my presence, or the new blueberry syrup that

I poured over your pancakes, for that matter."

I shut my eyes for a moment.

"That morning nearly broke me," I say. "And when you saw my eyes fogging up with tears, you promised me that you'd come home early that evening. You said you couldn't wait to get back to me. And I spent all day washing greens, peeling potatoes, and marinating beef just for you. Just to make your coming home early worth while."

I begin to pull the petals off of the rose, one by one, and place them on his grave.

"But you never came back, and for weeks, I thought it was a sign; you wanted nothing to do with me. I thought you didn't have time for me. You didn't want me...need me," I say.

"Jasmine, my counselor...my friend, told me that I had put too much of myself into our marriage. She said that I had "lost myself." But I didn't. I can't lose what I never had, right? Lately in this quest to find myself, all I've truly discovered is who I am not. It may take just a while longer to get to the essence of Lena, but I'm getting there. You'd be proud of me, Darius. You'd probably fall deeper in love, if you could see me now."

The birds continue to sing, as I drop my handful of rose petals onto Darius's grave. Some get picked up in the breeze and others lay beautifully, slightly covering his name.

I sit there for some time, reminiscing and thinking of all of the good times we had together. I think about when we were young and fresh out of college. We were care free and in love.

I laugh as I think about the time when we brought our first apartment together. We barely had any money, so for the first month we slept on a comforter on the floor. I think that's when we got the best sleep.

9

This isn't how I remember group therapy. Everyone is cracking up when I walk into the room. Since when did they sit around laughing? I creep into the circle, and sit down in one of the empty chairs. A woman who I do not recognize is sharing.

"We were waiting in that little boat for hours, and of course I was ready to go. It was hot as Hell and mosquitoes were biting me left and right, but my husband insisted that we stay. "This is the perfect time to catch a big one, Sally," he said."

The women are giggling and smiling, and I smile too as I look around at their happy faces.

"So we wait and wait and then sure enough his fishing rod jerked. That fish was trying to get off that rod so bad that it nearly pulled Mike off the boat. "Hold me up! Hold me up!" He was fussing and shouting in a way that I'd never seen him do before. I got scared!

"I jumped up and held onto him as hard as I could while he tried his best to reel the fish in, but that darn thing was so heavy that it started to pull us both! We were playing tug-of- war. Them people out in that lake must've thought we were crazy. "I got it, Sally!" he said, but before I knew it we were both floating in that water and to make it worse, I can't swim! I cussed my husband out bad that day," she said while laughing.

The women were nearly falling out of their seats. They needed a good laugh.

Jasmine wiped her eyes from the tears that came from laughing so hard. "Glad you could make it, Lena," she says.

"Me too," I say.

"Thank you for that story, Sally. Is there anyone else who wants to share anything?"

A few people are still giggling and chatting.

"I'll go," a woman says.

Jasmine nods for her to speak.

"Hi everyone. My name is Shannon."

"Hi, Shannon," we say.

We are all expecting another uplifting story, but we are reminded why we are here.

"Well, I lost my husband too. He's been gone for about four weeks," she says.

Her friend holds her hand while she speaks.

"I'm doing okay, I guess. It's just that I don't know what do with myself."

She pauses.

"My friends have been coming over and trying to get me to go out for dinner and things like that, but I can't. I just like to sit and think about him. I came here today because I wanted to see what other women who were going through the same thing as me look and feel like. I wanted to make sure that I wasn't the only one struggling."

"You're definitely not alone, Shannon," Jasmine says. "Each and every one of us has lost someone close to us, and though we may not all look sad today, we've had our days. But one day you'll leave out of here feeling greater than you've ever felt."

Shannon looks worn out, like she's been beating herself up every night. I look at her just as the women looked at me when I first shared. Now I understand why some of them had that look of pity in their eyes, and why I had seemed so familiar to them.

I know how hard this is for her. As a matter of fact, we all know. I've felt every last feeling that she feels right now. Half of these feelings, I am still trying to cope with.

The room is quiet.

"Anyone else have anything to share?"

On impulse, I raise my hand.

"Go ahead, Lena," Jasmine says.

"I'm not sure if anyone remembers me, but a little over a month ago I used to come to these sessions. I was completely broken then. I couldn't even get through the whole story behind my husband's death."

I begin to look at each woman's face. Some are sad and others look content.

"On the day that I shared, I left out of here with my mind made up, knowing that I would never come back. I didn't think that something like this would help me at all, but shortly after, I realized that talking to a group of people or at least someone who can relate to you makes all of the difference."

I look over to Jasmine.

"It's funny because I changed my calendar this morning, and it shocked me that five months have passed since my husband died, but I've realized that each day gets better. I'm laughing, smiling and singing. These are the simple things that I forgot about. There wasn't much time to sing and dance with my husband. His main focus was work and mine was to make sure he had everything that he needed. And although I am learning to enjoy this newfound time, there's still not a day that goes by when I don't think about him. There have been times when I've come across a few old photos of us and I immediately start to cry. Grieving takes time. This is just another step that helps us get there.

"With my husband gone, I thought that I had no real purpose. In my mind he was my purpose for living. But Jasmine taught me how to focus my attention on other things, like myself. And sure, when she first told me that I needed to think about myself during this time, I completely disagreed. It sounded selfish. How could I turn from my husband and only think about me?

"But I understand what she meant. Since I've known my husband, I've centered my attention on him. There was never any time for myself. Now I have all the time in the world. And I love it. I love how I can spend hours just sitting around doing nothing without having to worry about putting dinner on the stove or ironing my husband's clothes. I can breathe freely now. My time belongs to me and no one else."

The women applaud me as if I've jut won an academy award. Some are even crying. I can't even explain what I feel, but it feels good. I've got a feeling that I just touched someone's heart and gave her the courage to keep moving on just like Jasmine did for me. I never would've imagined that I had the ability to do that.

I stand as Jasmine walks over to me with open arms. As she hugs me, all of the women come over and cover us. I am in the center of love. The feeling of these women around me makes me strong. I feel invincible and deep down in my heart I know that they do too.

■ ■ ■

IMANI RASHIDA was born and raised in Baltimore, Maryland. She attended Baltimore City College high school, and graduated from Hampton University in 2012. She currently attends the University of Baltimore where she studies Publications Design, and works as editor for Baltimore FAM publications. *For Black Pearls* is her first published work.

www.ingramcontent.com/pod-product-compliance
Lightning Source LLC
Chambersburg PA
CBHW021450240626
47154CB00005B/1790